NOVEMBER

A MONTH OF ARTS AND CRAFTS AT YOUR FINGERTIPS!

Preschool–Kindergarten

Editors:
Mackie Rhodes
Jan Trautman

Artists:
Cathy Spangler Bruce
Pam Crane
Rebecca Saunders
Donna K. Teal

Cover Artist:
Kimberly Richard

www.themailbox.com

©2000 by THE EDUCATION CENTER, INC.
All rights reserved.
ISBN #1-56234-347-5

Manufactured in the United States

10 9 8 7 6 5 4 3 2 1

Table of Contents

Paper Plate Turkey

Rock this terrific little turkey right into your Thanksgiving celebrations. Invite each child to use her turkey in her play activities at school and then later as a holiday decoration at home.

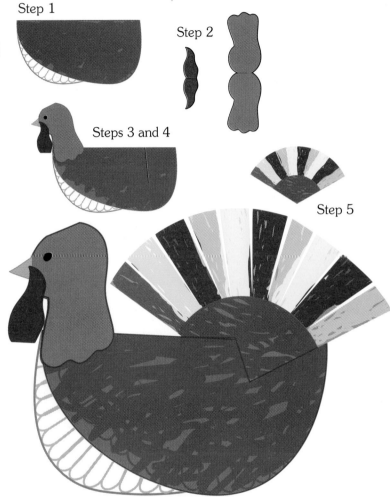

Materials (per child)

- 1 brown construction paper turkey head (pattern on page 22)
- 1 red construction paper turkey wattle (pattern on page 22)
- one 9" paper plate
- $\frac{1}{3}$ section of a paper plate (see Teacher Tips)
- orange construction paper
- brown tempera paint
- colored markers
- paintbrush
- scissors
- glue

Directions

1. Paint the back of the paper plate brown. After the paint dries, fold the painted plate (turkey body) in half.
2. Cut out the turkey head and wattle. Fold each piece on the dotted lines. Then cut out an orange triangle beak.
3. As shown, glue the beak and wattle onto the turkey head. Draw eyes on the head, and then glue the head onto the body.
4. Cut a slit in the turkey body as illustrated.
5. To make a turkey tail, color stripes on the rim of the paper plate section; then color the rest of that plate brown.
6. To create feathers, cut between each stripe on the tail.
7. Insert the tail into the slit on the turkey body.

Teacher Tips

- For every three students, precut one paper plate into thirds.
- If desired, glue wiggle eyes onto the turkey head.

Susan Bunyan—Dodge City, KS

Turkey Topper

Top off your students' Thanksgiving fun with these floppy turkey headbands.

Materials (per child)

1 yellow construction paper turkey body (pattern on page 23)
1 red construction paper turkey wattle (pattern on page 23)
1 orange construction paper turkey beak (pattern on page 23)
12" x 36" length of brown bulletin board paper
2 wiggle eyes
scissors
glue
pencil
stapler

Directions

1. Cut out all the turkey patterns. Glue the wiggle eyes, wattle, and beak onto the body.
2. Cut a three-inch-wide strip off one end of the brown paper to make a wing strip. Trim the length and the corners of the wing strip; then fringe-cut each end.
3. Glue the wing strip to the back of the turkey body.
4. To make the headband, fold the long brown paper into thirds; then make three equidistant cuts through all thicknesses as shown.
5. Round the corners of each section to create turkey tail feathers.
6. Glue the turkey body onto the headband.
7. Overlap the ends of the headband; then staple them together, sized to fit.

Susan Bunyan—Dodge City, KS

Teacher Tips

● If desired, wrap the fringed wing ends around a pencil and then release them to give the wings a feathery look. Curl the tail feathers in the same manner.

Tiny Turkey Basket

Load this little turkey basket with candy corn for a tasty take-home treat to gobble, gobble, gobble!

Materials (per child)

- feather tracers (pattern on page 22)
- small basket (approximately 1½" x 2½")
- 1" x 5" brown construction paper strip
- various colors of construction paper
- one 6" square of plastic wrap
- ribbon
- glue
- candy corn
- marker
- scissors

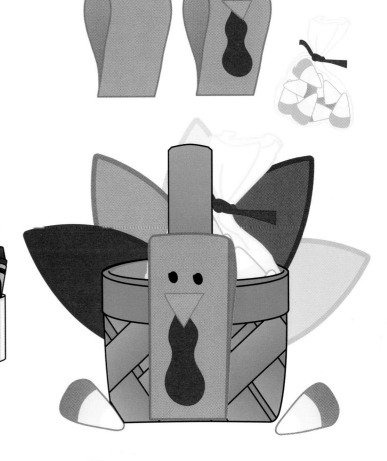

Directions

1. To make the turkey head, glue only the ends of the brown paper strip together, forming a raindrop-shaped loop.
2. Cut out an orange diamond beak and red wattle from construction paper. Glue these pieces onto the turkey head as shown. Draw eyes on the head.
3. Glue the head onto one side of the basket.
4. Trace the feather tracer onto several colors of construction paper and cut out the feathers.
5. Glue the feathers onto the side of the basket opposite the turkey head.
6. Wrap some candy corn in the plastic wrap and tie it with ribbon.
7. Nestle the wrapped candy in the turkey basket.

Susan Bunyan—Dodge City, KS

Teacher Tips

- To make feather tracers, cut out tagboard copies of the feather pattern on page 22.
- After youngsters eat their candy corn, suggest that they use their baskets as holiday napkin rings.

Sparkly Cornucopia

This cornucopia is a sparkling reminder of giving thanks. Display the cornucopias on a bulletin board for your students and class visitors to enjoy.

Materials (per child)

1 copy of each fruit pattern on page 24 (see Teacher Tips)
1 brown paper lunch bag
gold, red, purple, and orange glitter
green construction paper
glue
paintbrush
scissors

Directions

1. Cut out each fruit pattern.
2. Paint a fruit cutout with glue; then sprinkle it with the corresponding color of glitter. Repeat the process with each fruit.
3. Cut out a green stem or leaf (if appropriate) for each fruit. Glue the cutouts onto the fruit.
4. Fold the top of the bag down about one inch; then fold it down again.
5. Pull the bottom of the bag out, and then twist it to form a cornucopia as shown.
6. Glue the glittery fruit cutouts in the opening of the cornucopia.

Teacher Tips

● For each child, make a copy of each fruit pattern (page 24) as follows: a red apple, a yellow banana, an orange orange, and purple grapes.

● As an alternative (to cut back on glitter), mix each color of glitter into a different batch of white glue. Thin each mixture with water. Then paint each cutout with the corresponding color of glitter glue.

Kimberli Carrier—Nashua, NH

Turkey Candy Dish

Use this handy candy dish during your class Thanksgiving celebration. Afterward, invite each child to take her dish home to refill with a holiday treat for a special family member.

Materials (per child)

tagboard
construction paper in various
    colors (including brown)
1 wiggle eye
1 nut cup
pencil
scissors
glue
holiday treat (such as popcorn,
    candy corn, or a trail mix)

Directions

1. Trace your hand on the tagboard. Cut out the hand outline.
2. Tear an assortment of construction paper (including the brown) into small pieces.
3. Glue the brown pieces onto the palm and thumb of the hand cutout to resemble the turkey body.
4. Glue the other colors onto each finger to resemble turkey feathers.
5. Cut out a red wattle and orange beak. Glue these and the wiggle eye onto the turkey head.
6. Glue a nut cup onto the turkey body.
7. After the glue dries, fill the cup with a holiday treat.

Teacher Tips

● To encourage youngsters to tear the paper into small pieces, use construction paper scraps and strips.

● Pair students; then have each child trace her partner's hand. Help each child, as necessary, cut out her own hand outline.

Kathy Brand—Greenwood Lake, NY

Thankful Thoughts Picture Frame

Mom

me

Alan

Amber

Invite each child to highlight his illustrated thoughts of thankfulness with this unique picture frame. Then display all the pictures in art-gallery fashion. Periodically change the art in the frames to allow students to show off the many things for which they are thankful.

Materials (per child)

picture frame front and back
  (see Teacher Tips)
dried seeds and beans
craft glue
4" x 6" plain index card
crayons
tagboard strip

Directions

1. Color the picture frame front.
2. Glue seeds and beans onto the frame front to fill in or outline the printed designs or to create your own. Set the frame aside to dry.
3. Glue the frame front to the back along only the outer edges of three sides; then allow the glue to dry.
4. Illustrate the index card with a thankful thought.
5. Insert the picture into the open edge of the frame; then label a strip of tagboard with the artist's name. Display the art and name label together.

Teacher Tips
● For each child, copy the frame pattern (page 25) twice onto tagboard. Cut out both frames; then cut out the center of just one frame to use as the frame front.

Neat Napkin Holder

This pretty napkin holder is a fun *and* functional project to make. Encourage each child to fill her napkin holder at home and then display it on her family's Thanksgiving table.

Materials (per child)

1 large gelatin box (or a box of similar size)
flat tray
tempera paint
paintbrush
colored glue
tape
scissors
salt
napkins

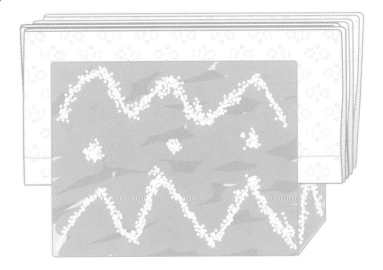

Step 1   Step 2

Directions

1. Open the flaps on both sides of the box. Cut off the longer flaps and the box top as shown.
2. Fold up the remaining flap on each side of the box; then tape it to the box to create a napkin holder.
3. Paint the napkin holder the color of your choice. Set it aside to dry.
4. Pour a layer of salt onto the tray.
5. Use your choice of glue colors to draw a design on one side of the napkin holder.
6. Press the design into the salt. Shake the excess salt off over the tray.
7. Repeat Steps 5 and 6 (on both sides) until the napkin holder is decorated as desired.
8. After the glue dries, fold and insert a stack of napkins into the holder.

Teacher Tips

- If desired, assemble the napkin holder (Steps 1 and 2) in advance.
- To make colored glue, add food coloring to a small bottle of glue. Replace the lid and shake well to mix.

Shake 'n' Stamp Placemat

What's shakin'? It's the fun foil shape stamps used to create this multisensory placemat! Laminate each child's placemat, and then send it home for her to use during her family's Thanksgiving meal.

Materials (per child)

2 sheets of 9" x 12" white construction paper
8" length of foil
1/4 cup uncooked rice
shallow trays of tempera paint colors
paintbrushes
glue
scissors

Directions

1. To make a shape stamp, put the rice in the center of the foil. Fold the foil as shown; then twist the ends together to create a handle. Gently mold the foil-covered rice into the desired shape, and then flatten the bottom of the stamper.
2. Use the shape stamp and the paint color of your choice to decorate one sheet of paper. Allow the paint to dry.
3. Fold the second sheet of paper in half lengthwise, and then unfold it.
4. Use a paintbrush to paint a simple design on one side of the paper; then fold the paper over the paint to create a mirror image of the design.
5. After the paint dries, cut the folded paper in half along the fold.
6. Glue each half onto the ends of the first paper to make a placemat.

Teacher Tips

- Group youngsters into pairs; then invite the partners to share their shape stamps with each other.
- To avoid creating paint pools on the placemat, dip each stamp into the paint, wipe off the excess paint on the tray rim, and then stamp the paper.

Native American Shaker

Add to your Thanksgiving celebration with this Native American shaker. Invite youngsters to dance and shake their shakers as you play a rhythmic drum pattern.

Materials (per child)

- 1 lidded plastic soda bottle (20 oz.) with bottom removed (see Teacher Tips)
- two 8" tissue paper squares in different colors
- permanent markers in assorted colors
- unpopped popcorn
- scissors
- hot glue
- stapler
- wide clear tape

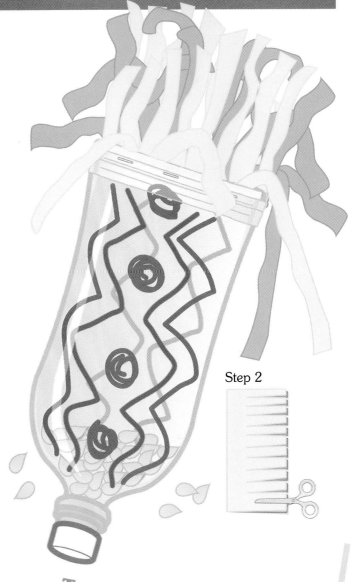

Step 2

Directions

1. Use permanent markers to decorate the bottle with a Native American design.
2. Stack the two tissue paper squares; then fold them in half. Fringe-cut the folded paper, leaving a 1 1/2-inch border of uncut paper on the folded end.
3. Pour two tablespoons of popcorn into the bottle; then staple the bottom of the bottle closed, trapping the intact ends of the fringed tissue paper inside.
4. To securely seal the contents of the shaker, wrap wide, clear tape around the stapled end of the bottle.

Teacher Tips

- In advance, cut off the bottom of the bottle. Cover the cut edges with tape to protect little hands. Then hot-glue the lid onto the bottle.
- Use a cotton swab dipped in alcohol to erase stray marks left by the markers.

adapted from an idea by Margaret Southard—Cleveland, NY

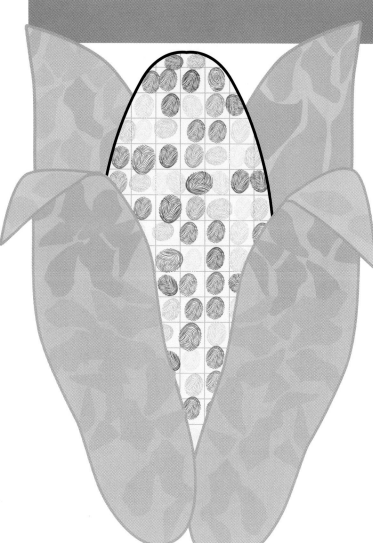

Indian Corn

Harvest a crop of this colorful corn to create a seasonal bulletin board. Use the display to inspire youngsters to brainstorm a list of foods made from corn. Then serve your class a popcorn snack.

Materials (per child)

1 manila corncob (pattern on page 26)
corn husk tracer (see Teacher Tips)
1 large brown paper bag
red, yellow, orange, and brown stamp pads
scissors
glue

Directions

1. Cut out the corncob pattern.
2. Using a different finger for each stamp pad color, fill the squares on the cob cutout with fingerprints.
3. Trace the corn husk four times onto the unprinted side of the bag; then cut out each outline.
4. Crumple each husk cutout, and then smooth it out.
5. Glue two husks to the back of the corn and two to the front as shown. Fold the front husks forward to create a three-dimensional effect.

Teacher Tips

- If desired, substitute brown construction paper or bulletin board paper for the husks.
- To make a husk tracer, cut out a tagboard copy of the husk pattern on page 26.
- As an alternative to colored stamp pads, use colored pencils to color the grid on the corn.

Susan Bunyan—Dodge City, KS

Walk Signal

Reinforce the international symbols for "Walk" and "Don't Walk" with this handy two-sided signal. Encourage youngsters to use their signs during dramatic play or outdoors in a modified game of Red Light, Green Light.

Materials (per child)

1 white construction paper copy of walk signal patterns (page 27)
1 sheet of yellow construction paper
1 large cratt stick
red and green crayons
black watercolor paint
water
paper towels
scissors
paintbrush
glue

Directions

1. Cut out each signal pattern. Color the symbol and word for "Walk" green; then color the "Don't Walk" symbol and words red.
2. Thoroughly cover each signal cutout with black watercolor paint. (If necessary, gently press a paper towel over each cutout to absorb beaded paint on the colored areas.) Set the cutouts aside to dry.
3. Fold the yellow paper in half to make a sign. Insert the craft stick between the two sides; then glue them together.
4. Glue a signal cutout onto each side of the sign.

Teacher Tips

● When coloring the symbols, have each child color heavily, pressing his crayon firmly against the paper.
● Write each child's name on his sign handle.

Twinkling Traffic Light

Enhance your students' dramatic-play activities and their knowledge of traffic rules with this traffic light project.

Step 1

Step 2

Step 3

Directions

1. Trace three circles (as shown) onto the tagboard.
2. Using the corn-syrup paint, paint the middle circle yellow, the bottom circle green, and the top one red. If desired, sprinkle a corresponding color of glitter on each circle. (Allow approximately two days for drying time.)
3. Next trace three circles onto the yellow paper and cut them out. Glue the remaining yellow piece onto the painted tagboard as shown.
4. Punch a hole above the red circle.
5. Attach a yarn hanger to the top of the traffic light.

Teacher Tips

● To make corn-syrup paint, stir food coloring into clear corn syrup until the desired color is achieved.

Patti Moeser—McFarland, WI

Railroad Crossing Signal

This freestanding sign will provide youngsters with lots of role-playing opportunities. Here comes a train—time to lower the arm! Ding-ding-ding!

Materials (per child)

- white poster board railroad patterns (pages 28 and 29)
- 2 cardboard egg-carton cups
- 1 plastic drinking straw
- 1 regular-size craft stick
- red crayon
- red construction paper
- black tempera paint
- 1 paper fastener
- scissors
- craft glue
- paintbrush
- hole puncher

Step 1   Step 2   Step 3

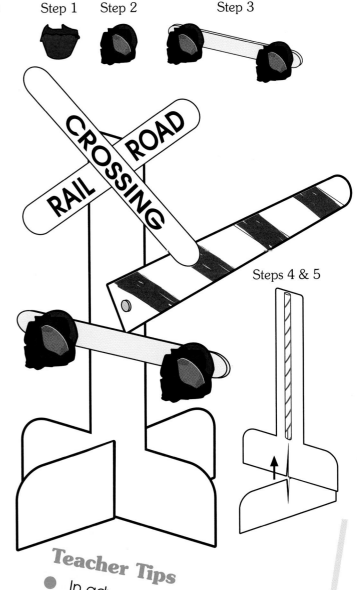

Steps 4 & 5

Directions

1. Paint the egg cups black; then let them dry.
2. Cut out two red circles. Glue each one in the bottom of an egg cup to resemble a railroad light.
3. Glue one light onto each end of the craft stick.
4. Cut out the railroad signal patterns. Cut slits in the post and base where indicated.
5. Align the straw with the top back edge of the post; then glue it on.
6. Cut out the crossbar patterns; then glue them together as shown. Glue the crossbar unit onto the top of the post.
7. Glue the lights onto the post where indicated.
8. Color red stripes on the arm cutout. Punch a hole in the arm and post where indicated.
9. After all the glue dries, attach the arm to the post with the paper fastener.
10. To assemble the signal, cut a short slit in the bottom of the straw; then fit the base into the post and straw slits.

Margaret Southard—Cleveland, NY

Teacher Tips

- In advance, prepare the post and base (Steps 4 and 5) for each child.
- To keep the arm in the raised position, slip it between the post and crossbars.

Bookmobile

Here's the perfect storage solution for the books made by your classroom authors. Keep these bookmobiles in your reading center for easy student access.

Materials (per child)

- bookmobile patterns (page 30)
- small photo of child
- 1 laundry-detergent box with lid removed
- 4 plastic milk-jug lids
- solid-colored gift wrap
- red and yellow sticky dots
- black tempera paint (optional)
- dishwashing liquid and paint-brush (optional)
- crayons
- scissors
- tape
- glue

Teacher Tips

- In advance, ask a volunteer to help wrap each individual box (Step 1).
- If desired, cut out the circle on the window pattern for each child.
- If desired, mix a few drops of dishwashing liquid with black tempera paint. Then use this mixture to paint the milk-jug lids.

Directions

1. Wrap the box with gift wrap. Fold the paper over the top opening and glue it down inside the box.
2. Cut out all the bookmobile patterns. Write your name on each label.
3. Color the characters on the front window cutout; then cut out the circle.
4. Back the window opening with your photo.
5. Glue the window, bumpers, and labels onto the box.
6. Attach two yellow sticky dot headlights and two red sticky dot taillights.
7. Glue the jug lids onto the box to make bookmobile wheels.

Margaret Southard—Cleveland, NY

Beautiful Bookmark

What makes this bookmark so beautiful? The uniquely personal statement that it makes about its creator! Encourage youngsters to use their personalized bookmarks at school during Children's Book Week (in November) and then later at home.

Materials (per child)

- a tagboard strip (to serve as the bookmark)
- small school photo of child
- a supply of magazines and catalogs
- construction paper scraps
- clear Con-Tact® covering
- ribbon
- scissors
- glue
- hole puncher
- black marker

Directions

1. Cut a designer edge around the photo; then glue it onto the bookmark.
2. Cut out magazine and catalog pictures representing your favorite things. Glue them onto the bookmark.
3. Cut a colorful shape out of construction paper. Label the shape with your name and then glue it onto the bookmark.
4. Cover the front of the bookmark with clear Con-Tact covering.
5. Write the title of a favorite book on the back of the bookmark.
6. Punch three holes along the bottom of the bookmark; then tie three lengths of ribbon to it.

Teacher Tips

- In advance, label each piece of tagboard with "My favorite book is…"

- If desired, invite students to bring in personal photos to use on their bookmarks.

Susan DeRiso—Barrington, RI

Shooting Star

Send youngsters' imaginations into outer space with this shimmering shooting star. Hang these stars from your ceiling; then invite each child to describe an imaginary ride on a shooting star.

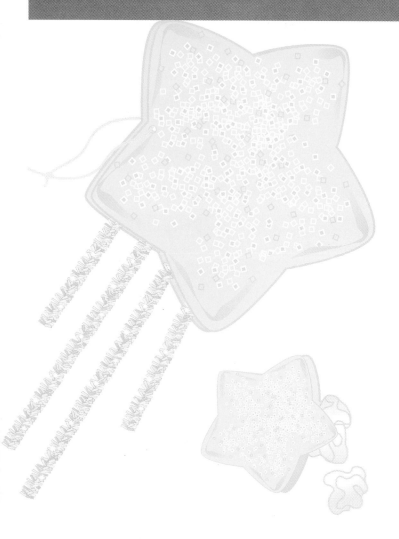

Materials (per child)

2 yellow construction paper stars
   (pattern on page 31)
2 gold sparkle pipe cleaners
tissue paper
gold glitter
scissors
glue
water
paintbrush
hole puncher
nylon thread

Directions

1. Cut out each star.
2. Paint each star cutout with water-thinned glue. Sprinkle glitter onto the glue; then set the stars aside to dry.
3. Cut one pipe cleaner into two different lengths. Cut the other pipe cleaner in half.
4. Glue the stars together along the back edges, leaving an opening between two points of the star.
5. After the glue dries, stuff crumpled tissue paper into the opening.
6. Insert the pipe cleaners between the two stars (as shown) to create the shooting star "streaks." Then glue the open edges together.
7. Punch a hole in the star; then tie a nylon hanger onto the star.

Margaret Southard—Cleveland, NY

Teacher Tips

● Mix water into white glue until it is thin enough to easily spread with a paintbrush.

● Have the child decide whether her star will shoot up, down, or across the sky; then punch the hole in the star so that it hangs as she desires.

Super Spaceship

Enhance your space unit with these personalized spaceships. Three, two, one...blastoff!

Materials (per child)

- white spaceship patterns (page 29)
- one 6-oz. foam cup
- 1/2 of a small foam plate
- small photo of child
- yarn
- crayons
- pencil
- scissors
- craft glue
- stapler

Directions

1. Cut out the spaceship patterns. Color all the patterns, then cut out the opening in the helmet. Back the opening with the photo.
2. Cut two 1 1/2-inch-wide strips from the straight edge of the plate half. Color one strip to resemble flames; then cut several long slits in the strip.
3. Staple the strip of flames onto the second strip (the wing strip) as shown.
4. Invert the cup and poke a hole in the bottom. Then poke both ends of a length of yarn through the hole and knot it to make a hanger for the spaceship (cup). Tape the knot to the inside of the cup.
5. Wrap the dome cutout around the yarn hanger to create the top of the spaceship. Glue the ends together; then glue the dome in place onto the spaceship.
6. Glue the window and label cutouts onto the spaceship.
7. Cut a 1 1/4-inch slit on opposite sides of the spaceship bottom; then insert the wings.

Susan DeRiso—Barrington, RI

Step 1

Step 2

Step 3

Step 4

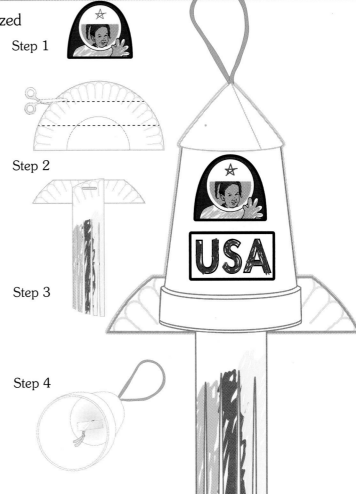

Teacher Tips

- Use pushpins to hold the window cutout in place while the glue dries.
- If desired, copy each child's photo; then use the copy in the spaceship window.

Bear Cave

Shh! Don't wake the hibernating bear! Use this activity to reinforce your unit on animal homes; then send each child home with his project to share the fun surprise with his family.

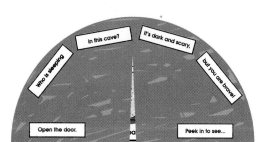

Directions

1. Paint the back of the paper plate brown.
2. After the paint dries, cut the plate in half. Starting at the middle of the straight edge, cut a long slit in one plate half (as shown).
3. Color and cut out the bear pattern; then cut out the text patterns.
4. Glue the bear cutout onto the front of the intact plate half. Glue the plate halves together (with the unpainted sides facing in).
5. Glue the text strips onto the front of the bear cave as shown.
6. After the glue dries, fold the front flaps up to reveal the surprise in the cave; then unfold them to hide the snoozing bear again.

Teacher Tip
- Use clothespins to hold the plates together while the glue dries.

Susan DeRiso—Barrington, RI

Migrating Geese

Wish our fine-feathered friends a safe flight as they migrate south for the winter. This unique activity is the perfect addition to your study of animals in the winter.

Materials (per child)

- geese text (pattern on page 32)
- 1 paper plate
- 1 sheet of blue construction paper
- brown tempera paint
- gray tempera paint
- white chalk
- scissors
- paintbrushes
- glue

Directions

1. Cut the plate (similar to the one shown above) to resemble a tree.
2. Paint the tree brown.
3. Cut several pairs of short strips from the rim scraps of the paper plates. Paint the strips gray.
4. When the paint is dry, glue the tree to the blue construction paper.
5. Arrange the short strips to resemble geese. Then glue the rim of each wing to the background.
6. Cut out the text and glue it onto the picture.
7. Use chalk to draw snow on the ground, on the tree, and in the sky.

Teacher Tips

- If gray paint is not available, mix white and black paint together.
- To keep the chalk from smearing, spray a light coat of hairspray over the completed picture.

adapted from an idea by Susan DeRiso—Barrington, RI

Turkey Patterns
Use with "Paper Plate Turkey" on page 3.

head

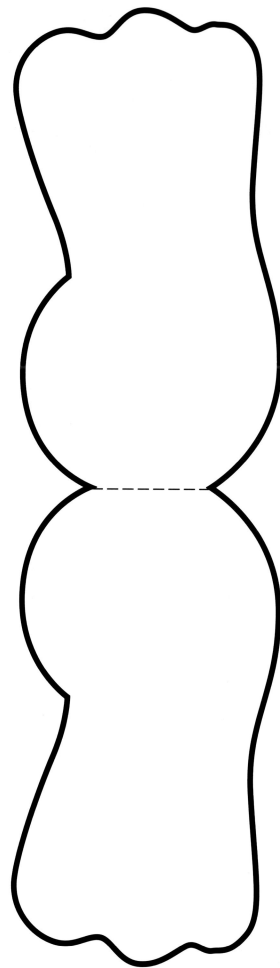

wattle

Feather Pattern
Use with "Tiny Turkey Basket" on page 5.

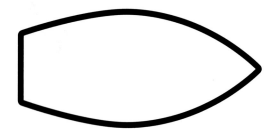

body

wattle

beak

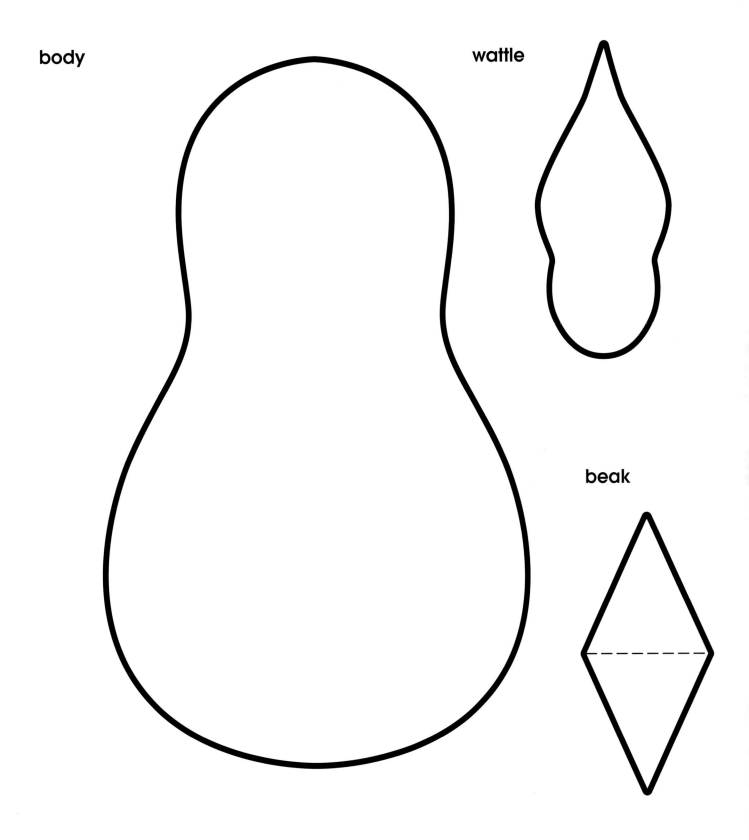

Fruit Patterns
Use with "Sparkly Cornucopia" on page 6.

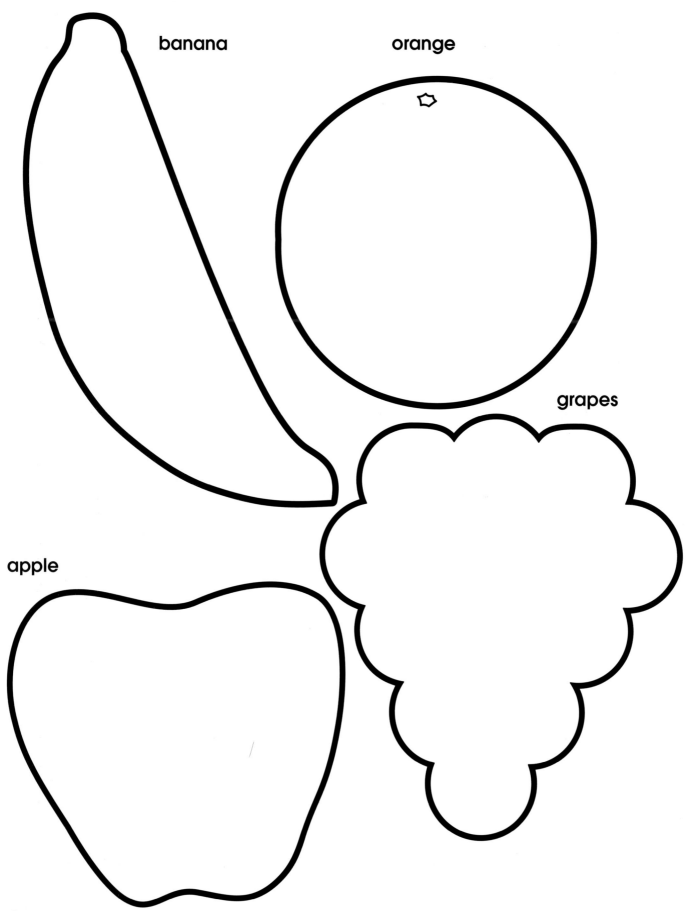

banana

orange

grapes

apple

25

Corn Patterns
Use with "Indian Corn" on page 12.

corn   **husk**

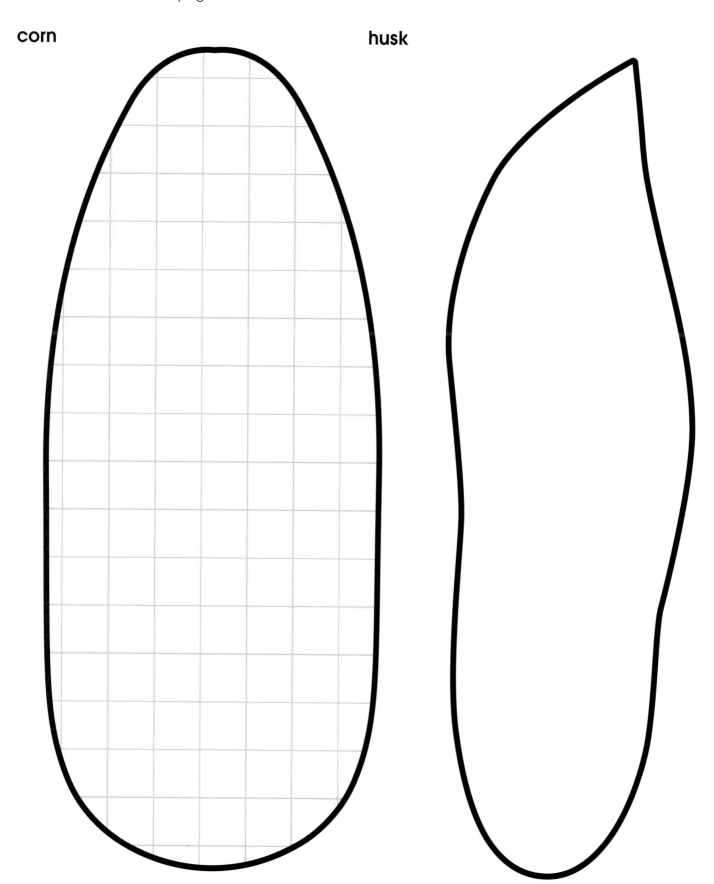

Railroad Signal Patterns

Use with "Railroad Crossing Signal"
on page 15.

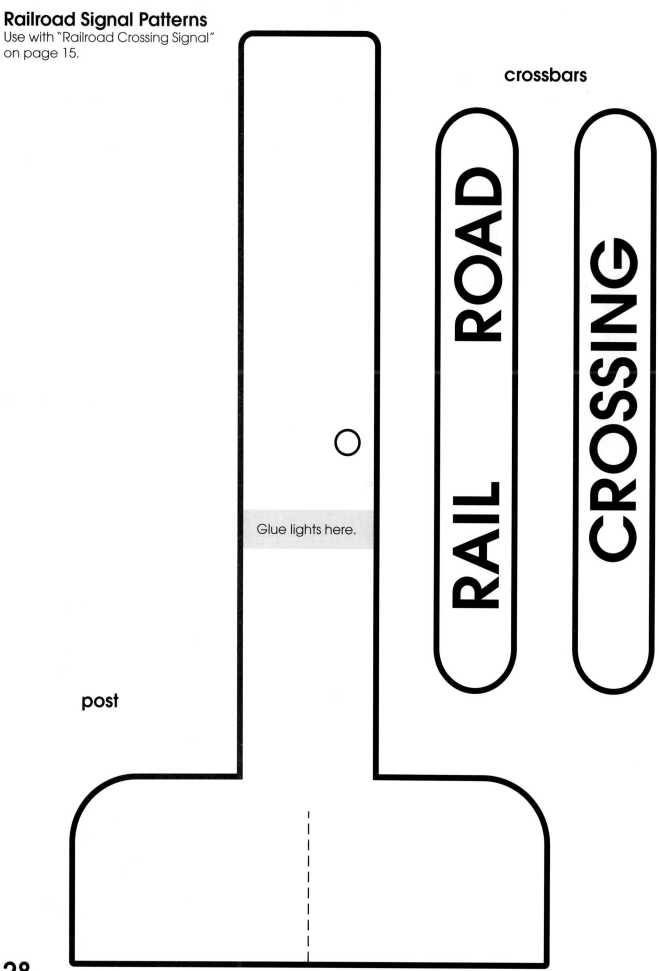

crossbars

ROAD
RAIL

CROSSING

Glue lights here.

post

©2000 The Education Center, Inc. • *November Monthly Arts and Crafts* • Preschool/Kindergarten • TEC1050

arm

base

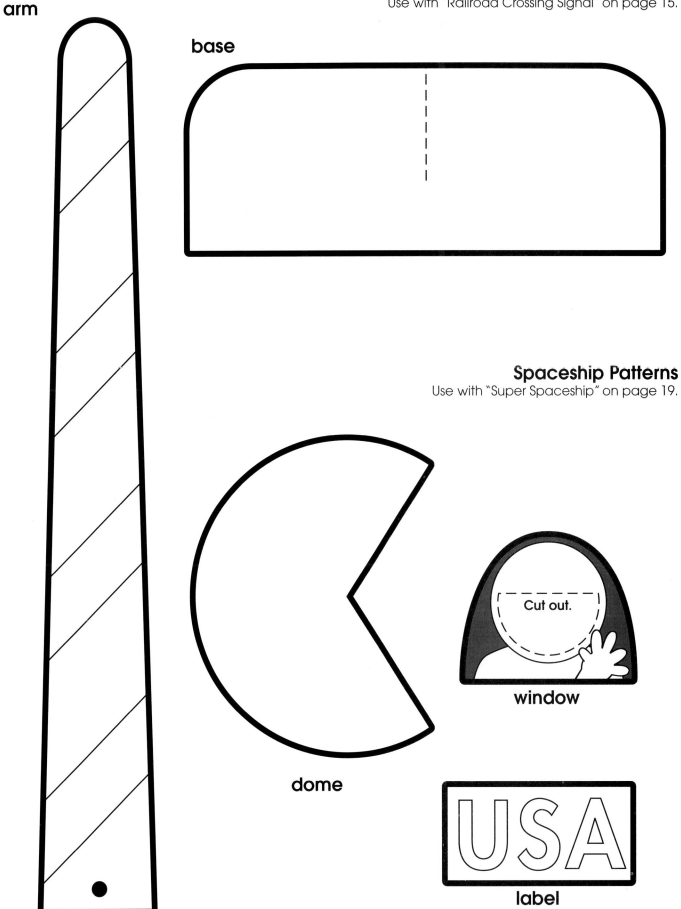

Cut out.

window

dome

USA

label

29

Bookmobile Patterns
Use with "Bookmobile" on page 16.

window

_____'s

BOOKMOBILE

's

BOOKMOBILE

labels

back bumper

I ♥ 2 READ

front bumper

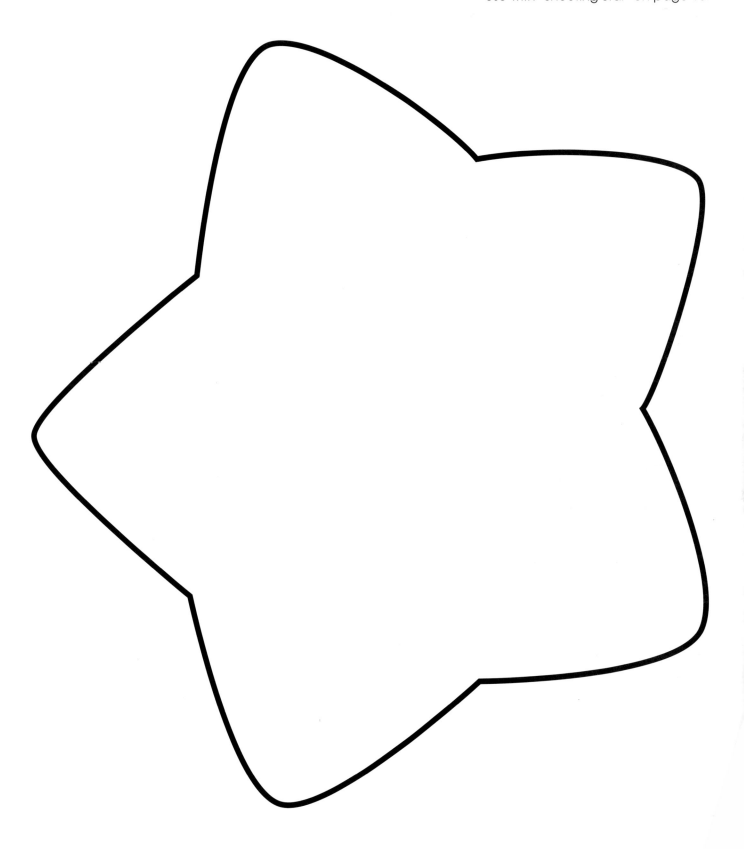

Bear and Text Patterns
Use with "Bear Cave" on page 20.

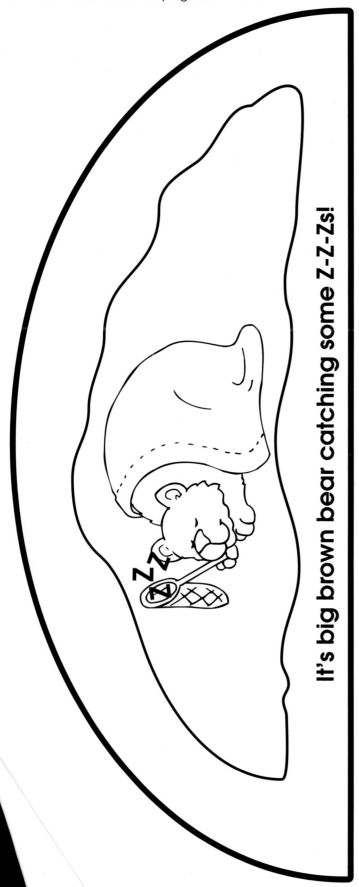

It's big brown bear catching some Z-Z-Zs!

Who is sleeping
in this cave?
It's dark and scary,
but you are brave!
Open the door.
Peek in to see...

Geese Text Pattern
Use with "Migrating Geese" on page 21.

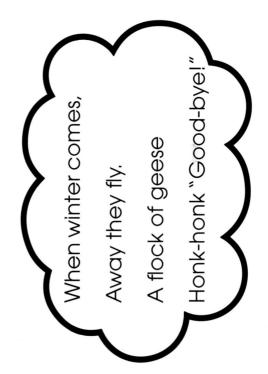

When winter comes,
Away they fly.
A flock of geese
Honk-honk "Good-bye!"